*To a wonderful friend
with L*

# Spiritual Alchemy

## POETIC MESSAGES OF DIVINE SPIRITUAL HEALING

*Janine Palmer*

# BY JANINE PALMER (SILVER MOON) CHT
# A JP SILVER MOON SERIES

# OTHER BOOKS BY JANINE PALMER

MAIN BOOKS:

Divine Heretic – Standing Holy
Divine Heretic – In Christ Consciousness
Divine Heretic – Sacred Scribe
Divine Heretic – Mystical Fire
Divine Heretic – Alchemist
Divine Heretic – Hierophant
Divine Heretic – Hidden Keys
Divine Heretic – Wordsmith
Divine Heretic – Song of the Seraphim

JP SILVER MOON SERIES:

Magic Quill, Sacred Sword
Fire & Thunder of the Bard
Mystical Whispers of the Soul
Mystical Whispers of the Scribe
Quicksilver Ink
Owl Feather, Sacred Scribe
Recalling the Mystery, Goddess of Arc
On Winged Destrier
Points of the Queen's Crown
Whispers of the Woods
Extracting Wisdom from Experience

Soul Speak, Mystical Heart
Divine Illumination

GENRE SPECIFIC BOOKS
(Material Pulled from Main Books)

Energy Healing Wisdom
Spiritual Healing Wisdom
Divine Healing Wisdom
Rising Above Dogma
For Romance
Heart Speak
Romantic Reflections
Book of Worthiness
Apocalypse of Worthiness
Scriptures of Worthiness
Shamanic Energy Medicine
Sacred Shamanic Whispers

# DEDICATION

This book is dedicated to my family with deep love and to all the people who inspired me to write and to all poets and writers. The poetry contained herein is an acknowledgement to the healing powers of writing.

Writing about the importance of processing and releasing emotions becomes artistic expression. Energy needs to flow. These tales are about releasing those blocks. Trust the process of unfolding and spiritual evolvement.

Blessings, love and light.

Janine Palmer (Silver Moon) CHT

# FORWARD

This little book reflects glimpses of experience and the wisdom gained from them. It reflects wounds, and the effects of the wounded who wound. It speaks of energy healing and forgiveness. It speaks of spiritual alchemy and the ascension of the spirit and the soul. It speaks of opening the door of the heart to love.

It speaks of battle scars and shedding skins and shells. It speaks of sacred temples and the fire of transformation. It speaks of rising above and moving beyond judgment, the spiraling, higher path to freedom through love and healing and releasing what does not serve. It speaks of the power of forgiveness. It speaks of things mystical and sacred. It speaks of magic.

It speaks of angels and dragons and divine love. It speaks of mirrors, treasures, keys and the mystical. It speaks of shadow and perspectives. It speaks of spirit, heart, soul and light. It speaks of deeper truth beyond belief and hidden keys. It basically shares the depth of love revealed by life experiences.

# INTRODUCTION

What is shared in my writings often comes from wisdom gained through experiences, sometimes very grueling experiences. What is shared is also tools and knowledge gained from many healing modalities and certifications as well as much study of religions, religious scholars and spiritual teachers.

My work is for the purpose of reminding people of their worthiness and rising above judgement as far as condemnation of others due to lack of compassion or understanding.

What I write often comes from what I've learned from experiences and I share it for awareness along with tools for strengthening and healing. It's for sharing knowledge and wisdom gained through experience along with tools I've learned from training in different types of energy healing.

It has been part of my healing process to write and give talks about transforming lower vibrational energy to higher vibrational energy.

Everything is about interpretation or misinterpretation and perspective or misperspective. I have found being able to change perspective to be a key skill in bringing about positive change.

These little stories offer information about healing self and stepping away from toxic energies. Everyone interprets them differently. What I speak of comes from being destroyed and shattered. Some of what I write comes from the parts of me which survived and endeavored to tell the tales and share what I learned.

JP Silver Moon

NOTE:

This book speaks of deep spiritual perspectives, including wisdom from ancient scriptures, which some people might be open to consider for deep generational healing. Some of the content is esoteric and deeply spiritual which some might be interested in reading, knowing or remembering.

This book might speak to true spiritual seekers who are open to perspectives other than the ones they currently 'believe'. It's written for those who are on the path of remembering and restoring their connection to their own worthiness, or who wish to be.

JP Silver Moon

# CONTENTS

# Sacred Temple

Within your temple is stored great and ancient wisdom. It whispers to you. Do you hear it?

*Sacred Temple*

As you awaken to your truth, your inner beauty, and your light, illusion will begin to fade.

*Sacred Temple*

What is sacred, is the love you feel but cannot describe, which whispers to you of home.

*Sacred Temple*

He knew how to communicate
with her. That was enough.

*Sacred Temple*

Bathed in moonbeams
and starlight, I felt peace.

*Sacred Temple*

By his confidence, his bravery, his curiosity and his intention to know more about her, he did.

She respected in him those qualities which were also in her.

We recognize and are drawn to people by vibration.

*Sacred Temple*

Sacred is his divine energy. Sacred is when he honors her by his words and actions toward her and about her, in her presence or in her absence.

*Sacred Temple*

# Glimpses of Soul

When he hugged me, a primal sound of relief sounded from deep within his chest and I felt my presence there with him was a beautiful thing for him, that made me feel deeply happy.

*Glimpses of Soul*

Sometimes when he hugged me,
he wouldn't let go. I loved that.

*Glimpses of Soul*

His kind and supportive words chipped away at the protective walls she'd built around herself.

He chiseled his way into her heart with kindness and attentiveness.

*Glimpses of Soul*

People's behavior and treatment toward you shows you who is supposed to be present in your little court of miracles, as does your behavior toward others.

*Glimpses of Soul*

Those who are courteous, kind, thoughtful, respectful and attentive, clear or create a path to a place to be welcome in your energetic space. Those who don't, don't.

People show you who they are. Issues will always reveal themselves, then it's up to you to determine what is good for your energy, or not.

Anyone who is a taker, who withdraws and drains your energy without making deposits of the same, is destructive, whether they know it or not. Take care of you.

*Glimpses of Soul*

Sometimes we're tired of what life really is or seems to be, because it's not what we think it should be.

That is an invitation to find the beauty and the blessings where you currently are and be in gratitude for them before you can move forward.

A change in perspective opens new windows and doors.

*Glimpses of Soul*

To that infrequent engagement of interaction,
that inconsistent presence of good manners and
that ongoing lame and blatant lack of
communication, I say, 'Bollocks and no thanks'.

*Glimpses of Soul*

# Mystical & Sacred

Compassion which is whispered from Grace and delivered through love and kindness, is sacred beauty and power in action.

*Mystical & Sacred*

Sacred is the love he whispers to
me which no one can understand
as deeply as I do.

*Mystical & Sacred*

The sacred shared by the wise ones
is for the collective, as the collective
is sacred, even if they don't remember.

*Mystical & Sacred*

Sometimes people revere and give more importance to the dead than they do the living.

Living in the past is like in invisible cell, to an idea, ideology or memory of something.

We create in the now.

*Mystical & Sacred*

I wouldn't be able to recognize the divine beauty in another if it wasn't also in myself.

*Mystical & Sacred*

Grace is humble and doesn't pretend. It just is.

*Mystical & Sacred*

In the realm of benevolent
flying dragons and beautiful
unicorns, part of me waits.

*Mystical & Sacred*

# Divine Wisdom

Each of us has gifts where we have knowing and each of us has had experiences others don't know about which affect how we function and how we feel.

We have different perspectives from different experiences. Everyone is our teacher, good or bad.

*Divine Wisdom*

Command respect through
integrity. If it is absent, walk on.

*Divine Wisdom*

And sometimes we are fooled
by our own thoughts.

*Divine Wisdom*

He was once my best and truest friend. Then he became one of the greatest challenges I'd ever faced, including my nemesis, for a time.

Teachers come in all disguises. Forgiveness is a super power and a master key, and so is my laughter.

*Divine Wisdom*

Everything is up to, or down to, interpretation. Nobody sees things from exactly the same viewpoint or perspective, as they are looking at different aspects of it from the results and effects of different experiences.

We are all at different levels of woundedness or healing.  We are at different levels of programming and conditioning. Which taints the lenses we are seeing through.

*Divine Wisdom*

Most people have their programmed ideologies of how people should behave or not, about what boxes they should fit into, due to interpretation and more importantly, misinterpretation.

So then if someone doesn't comply with those matrix codes of ignorance, many people think they have a license to judge, belittle, find fault and condemn, as if they were god. And it feeds their egos, on an individual and collective level.

And they don't see it because they 'believe' they are right. There comes a point on this gauntlet of an earth journey to move beyond the limitations of belief, and into knowing. Amen.

*Divine Wisdom*

I have learned much about myself
through others and what they have
shown me or reflected back to me.

I have also learned to recognize when
something being projected at me isn't
mine or about me.

*Divine Wisdom*

Don't focus too long on what you perceive to be negative in a way that keeps you stuck in a negative state. Look more deeply into it. What did you learn from it?

How did you become stronger or wiser because of it? Did you discover a deeper element of compassion? Did you discover the power of forgiveness yet?

Did you get in touch with yourself on a deeper level? Did you shed any skins or shells? Did you learn to cut cords? Did you learn to take your power back?

*Divine Wisdom*

People should never make assumptions. So many people constantly believe thoughts and fears which are not true and suffer greatly because of it.

Don't forget the world is surrounded in illusion and the effects of misunderstanding. There comes a time to part the mists.

*Divine Wisdom*

# Energy Healing

We struggle with relationships here,
due to wounds, ours and/or theirs.
Heal the wounds, find your bliss.

*Energy Healing*

Your unattended wounds might not be a perfectly valid reason to starve your partner or abuse your friends. Healing 101.

*Energy Healing*

Sometimes when you are feeling disconnected, it helps to go out in nature. Put your feet or hands on the earth or grass.

Deep breath work also helps. A few minutes of meditation to visualize releasing what doesn't serve you then replacing it with love.

*Energy Healing*

Sometimes you can't 'get rid' of things. Rather, you need to heal them or transmute them. It's called Alchemy. Change it into love, through love.

*Energy Healing*

One day she posted this on her Facebook page.

'Dear Haters, I'm sorry you are suffering and blaming it on others. Beware of how it affects others who have nothing to do with what you carry.

I hope one day you can transmute that hatred to into love.'

*Energy Healing*

Prescription from Love:

Gratitude
Compassion
Silence
Release

Repeat as needed...

*Energy Healing*

To Create a Space for Healing

Perspectives of who you are or what you're like, differ from person to person. Some people are in energies of resentment, anger, sadness, pain, grief, victim-hood, judgment and jealousy, which they may or may not even realize. If they judge you, resent you, fear you, or are jealous in any way, their perspectives will be skewed until their energy and thoughts improve by their own healing.

The problem is we often get stuck in programs we run which are fed by lower vibrational thoughts, most of which are not even true. If wounded people share their jacked up views with others, the toxicity get spread around. Many believe falsehoods and then react to them. Each individual reflects their level of consciousness, woundedness or healing, by their actions.

That is why it is so important not to take things personally so we don't take on lower vibrational issues. Reacting to it feeds it and gives it energy or power. Many of us have the ability to communicate without explosive reactions, many do not.

If only one person is capable of honorable communication without being disrespectful, then nothing is going to get resolved.

Egos like to believe they are always right. Old wounds, like pressurized volcanoes, often explode and spew venomous lava. Consciousness allows us to realize there might be something going on we don't fully understand. To acknowledge that is a type of freedom. It frees us from the shackles of egoic falsehood to create a space for healing.

This is not an easy lesson to learn, but non-reaction equals strength and power. When we allow ourselves to get drawn into this drama due to a need to defend ourselves, it reflects unhealed wounds in ourselves. There are times when we will need to stand up for ourselves, but its best to do it in a way that doesn't create more strife.

Writing down experiences and feelings is very healing. Honor yourself for the divine being you are, even if you don't recognize it yet, and even if and especially if others do not see it because they are swimming the effects of their own unhealed wounds. Peace and blessings.

*Energy Healing*

# Spiritual Healing

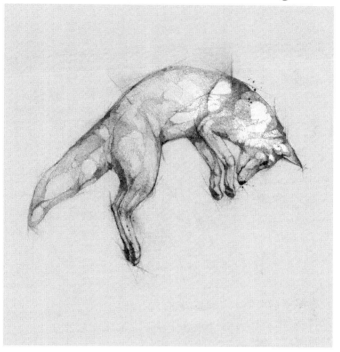

Invite yourself to find and follow the root to something that needs to be healed in you... for transformation.

*Spiritual Healing*

Amen to remembering and
awakening to the truth of
love beyond the veil.

*Spiritual Healing*

What I let go of
created space for
freedom.

*Spiriual Healing*

We are trying to understand or remember what has been veiled from us since we entered the adventure.

*Spiritual Healing*

We've all heard people talking shit about another, and what does that reflect about the one who does it?

*Spiritual Healing*

Your own love is the
most healing force.

*Spiritual Healing*

It's a big job healing the ego and the inner child, but the rewards are powerful.

*Spiritual Healing*

# Fire of Transformation

Certain things can seem utterly devastating, until we rise out of the ashes burning brighter and hotter and more powerful than the flames which burned us.

*Fire of Transformation*

Everything is fuel for the fire.
What needs to burn?

*Fire of Transformation*

What agenda does anyone or anything have which would cause you or anyone else to hate? Does anything cause it, like we have no control over it? Or is it a choice and what is it reflecting on a deeper level if we were to look more closely at ourselves?

How does hatred serve you or keep you stuck? Does anyone make us hate or is it reflecting something unresolved within? What power and peace lies beyond the realm of hate?

When we are balanced, we don't react in volatile ways. We don't feel the need to. The reactions are from triggers. The triggers are showing us what wants and needs to be released, but we have to move out of the trap of blame and perceived victimhood.

How powerful we are when we can observe without extreme reaction and/or pain and blame. The pain is/was a teacher. It doesn't need to be in charge and shouldn't be. When we take our power back, the pain won't be in charge.

Things need to move through us and not stay stuck, for us to experience balance and well-being.

Take the wisdom gained, release the rest. What do you carry which might cause you to be out of balance? What needs to be released?

*Fire of Transformation*

The reason I am so passionate about healing and stopping hatred or shining a light on it, is because of how I was harmed, temporarily, by that vile energy.

If you knew my stories, you would understand. We don't always feel what another feels, so we don't and can't really know. That is where empathy and compassion comes into play.

*Fire of Transformation*

Some people like to learn and are open enough to do so. Sometimes learning is unlearning.

Sometimes learning is being brave enough to step out of programming and conditioning and the rusty shackles of ego and throw that old hatred and resistance into a nice bright fire.

Shedding skins and shells to find the truth within. Woo hoo!!

*Fire of Transformation*

The divine fires which forged you
always burn brightly within you.

Fire of Transformation

# Spiritual Alchemy

We have particular connections with people for a reason. We have connections but they don't stay as a particular thing because things are always changing and evolving, moving and flowing in and out of existence. It's there for a moment, but it's never quite what it seems.

*Spiritual Alchemy*

Sometimes friends can help us feel better. Sometimes we have to do it ourselves. Only we can reach deep enough into our own depths to locate and remove the weeds that are choking us on some level.

It is our responsibility to water, feed and nurture those beautiful parts of ourselves if we want them to blossom. Friends might help show us where our healing work is needed most, through the good and the bad. It's probably why they are on our path.

*Spiritual Alchemy*

Unfortunately much of the world labors under debilitating misperceptions. We do NOT have pure knowledge about what we perceive and through illusion. We 'believe' things which are not true. Viewpoints are skewed and they keep people stuck in suffering and fighting.

We are here to learn from our choices, decisions, actions and reactions, good or bad, wrong or right, in the realm of duality until we learn to rise above or move beyond. We cannot rise above or move beyond anything if we are attached to ideologies and taking sides. God, Creator, Source, Great Spirit. Love is in everyone and everything, however we understand or misunderstand it.

We are here to learn to love one another and we don't do it by attacking, judging and holding onto hold pain, much of which was created from falsehood, because we reacted to something we didn't understand. And from fear and ego we lash out and attack, unknowingly keeping ourselves stuck. IT IS TIME FOR ANCESTRAL HEALING AND IT MUST BE DONE THROUGH LOVE.

*Spiritual Alchemy*

It doesn't matter at what age you open and awaken, to your truth within, it just matters that you do.

Along the way it's also important to be aware of, honor, and heal your inner child. We get caught up in life and distracted by so many things.

Don't forget the tender, beautiful parts of yourself. Take time to play and take time to heal.

*Spiritual Alchemy*

I have a very enlightened friend who is well studied in Christian scripture, to the point that he is no longer led around by misinterpretations of it. He still loves and honors Jesus, however.

He made a comment that he'd been told by someone that he was the most inappropriate man of God they had ever met. Really?

Let's look into this fallacy a little more deeply. My response to that, from my learning and limited perspective to date was as follows:

I said, "That's because they cannot see past their own limiting, conditioning, to truth when it's right in front of them. Nothing of God is inappropriate. What is inappropriate is judgment and the stench of 'Holier-than-Thou' attitudes.

They disrespect God in a way to even say that, but then they might worship a lower god and not even realize it, so that might explain their childish comments of ignorance."

I said, "Keep doing God's work Brother, even if the sleeping, wearing fake badges of 'Christianity', don't see it."

*Spiritual Alchemy*

The process of transformation is the journey. Awakening to wisdom is the wonder. It's an exercise in remembering. Embracing love is the power. Recognizing and releasing what's false is the key.

*Spiritual Alchemy*

# Worthiness & Wings

He's not interested in what speaks to her heart and soul, therefore, he can't really speak to her on her level of what love and truth is to her.

*Worthiness & Wings*

They used to play you and put you down, but it doesn't work anymore because you've grown stronger.

They might still try, but they won't win from that lower energy. They are tests, my darling, and you are doing fine.

*Worthiness & Wings*

Angels are always around,
even when they are not seen
or recognized.

*Worthiness & Wings*

Empathy for another who is suffering is so important. To care. To act. To lift. To listen. To hear. To whisper encouragement. It is empowering to the giver and to the receiver.

And then there are those who feed off of the suffering they create. Those who would kick you when you are down and suffering. They don't seem to see it or they don't care, because they are suffering too. They are tests to rise above.

*Worthiness & Wings*

For some sad reason he didn't think he was good enough for her, so he held back and wasn't able to give her what she needed.

How falsehood through illusions destroys.

*Worthiness & Wings*

Is there anything unhealed in you? Is there anything unhealed in me? Is there anything unhealed, known or unknown, in any or every person on this planet? Is it part of our learning journey?

Is it easier to blame someone or something else than it is to look more deeply into the parts of us which are triggered and take responsibility for acknowledging what needs attention within ourselves?

Blaming things outside of ourselves is typically a convenient distraction which doesn't serve our forward movement.

We can recognize when something is wrong or not working and then it is up to us to determine what we need to do to make a change for our greater good, even if it is changing our perspective.

*Worthiness & Wings*

She was hypnotic, like the flame of a candle moving ever so gently within the Mystery.

*Worthiness & Wings*

He had a magnetism about him that
was like reading a secret love letter
you just found hidden away somewhere.

*Worthiness & Wings*

# Blessed Be Our Magic

Magic is the way he looks at
me like there is no one he sees
the way he sees me.

*Blessed Be Our Magic*

Magic is the depth of love and the gentle, selfless way we express it.

*Blessed Be Our Magic*

Love yourself because you are a magnificent being of Light. It's time to remember your divinity. What gifts do you have to share with humanity?

In what way does your light shine brightest? Share that light with others. This is how we reflect the love of our Creator.

*Blessed Be Our Magic*

We're all magic and that magic is love. We create with it. We came in with that magic. It's who we are.

*Blessed Be Our Magic*

He was a special kind of light that shined on her in such a spectacular way. Like the way sunlight shines into a stone temple on the Solstice.

*Blessed Be Our Magic*

When the light was dim,
I had to focus more.

*Blessed Be Our Magic*

A type of romance flowed from her that was the stuff of fairy tales. It was like a rare wine, locked away and not many had the key to access it.

*Blessed Be Our Magic*

Her energy was like the familiar fragrance of a flower. You couldn't remember where you'd smelled it before, but you couldn't get enough of its intoxicating essence.

*Blessed Be Our Magic*

# Deeper Truth

People have reasons for what they do which others aren't aware of, including soul contracts, whether completed or not, and then there's free will.

*Deeper Truth*

What they showed me wasn't truth.
It wasn't recognized as truth by my
soul, so I left it behind.

*Deeper Truth*

When you trust, is it like giving your power away to expectations? Is it different than being trustworthy?

*Deeper Truth*

In the aftermath of awareness, truth appeared.

*Deeper Truth*

Sometimes truth flickers in and out,
but when we know it's truth, it stays.

*Deeper Truth*

So many want to blame or are in the habit of blaming and focusing on (perceived) fault and negativity. It's a trap. Invite yourself to take your power back!

*Deeper Truth*

Truth whispers. It sings.
It's familiar. It's safe.

*Deeper Truth*

When you encounter truth,
your perceptions change.

*Deeper Truth*

# Mirror, Mirror

On the road back to myself, I met
you, and in you are an aspects of me.

*Mirror, Mirror*

We go through processes of healing deep pain, through observation and limited perspective. We feel through experience until we learn to detach and rise above.

Through certain trying experiences we find great strength and hopefully in the process, we don't allow things which appear to be devastating, to have power over us.

*Mirror, Mirror*

When I awoke, the dream
became even lovelier.

*Mirror, Mirror*

Look beyond, beneath, and in between. If he caused so many people to be able to find their voice, use their voice, and finally speak their truth, then couldn't that be viewed as a 'good' thing? Even if they blame him for what he did or didn't do?

Things that appear to be 'bad' often lead us two things which are 'good'.

It's time to take the blinders off and shut the old programs down. What do you see happening? What you really see? Or do you? There are many things out there trying to distract us and keep us fighting.

Just saying.

*Mirror, Mirror*

When compassion is
present, God is present.

*Mirror, Mirror*

All judgment is self-judgement. It reflects the wounded parts in us.

If a person 'A' tries to put person 'B' down (judgement), it reveals a lot about person 'A's unresolved or unhealed issues.

To get to a place of not feeling the need to judge another person is a higher vibrational place to function from. It's freer. It flows. It means ego isn't in charge.

*Mirror, Mirror*

Sometimes it helps to talk about mistakes or wrong paths and what was learned from the experiences. But not to be used against someone when they are trying to rise above and improve. They are growing. We grow out of skins and shells.

Some people are just mean and they'll kick the stool out from under you. But remember, they will have to experience the ripple effects of everything they create through their choices, decisions, actions and reactions. The mistakes are how we learn.

*Mirror, Mirror*

# Battle Scars & Shedding Skins

The behavior of people around can be exhausting and draining at times. There are times we must step away for our own self-care and well-being.

Even in a family dynamic we can learn how not to get drawn into and triggered. We have to function in our own little world or vibrational space, even in the same house.

Lots of grounding and clearing is helpful to keep our own energy field clear and well.

*Battle Scars & Shedding Skins*

Some people do like to fling their shite at us but we are not targets unless we allow it. It's a great thing when we step into and stand in our power.

*Battle Scars & Shedding Skins*

It sucks when we chase away those we love the most due to the behaviors which stem from our unattended and unhealed wounds.

*Battle Scars & Shedding Skins*

Many wallow in deep pain which they don't know how to release, or they refuse to. It becomes part of their identity. Sometimes they try to drag you into their pit, but you have wings.

*Battle Scars & Shedding Skins*

Having expectations of others creates suffering and the need for healing in us and/or them.

*Battle Scars & Shedding Skins*

We need to become seekers, as Jesus taught. Belonging to a particular denomination or sect and thinking it is the only 'right' one, is one of the fastest ways to remain stuck, controlled, in the dark, and in the grip of ego.

That is not seeking. That is adopting and placing oneself in the illusion of a comfort zone. That is a dogmatic box and self-installation of blinders due to fear and ego.

What if we became true seekers to discover, learn and remember the deeper meanings of Christ's teachings?

*Battle Scars & Shedding Skins*

You can tell so much about people
by the vibration of their comments.

*Battle Scars & Shedding Skins*

# Treasure & Keys

I am grateful for people who have stood up for me, spoken up for me, guided me and taught me, even by their heinousness which made me wiser and stronger.

I am grateful for those who were and are compassionate, for those rare ones who don't judge. I am grateful for those who know me and reflect back to me things I need to see.

*Treasure & Keys*

In between the layers of life experiences
are stored vast treasures for us to share
at the times they are needed.

*Treasure & Keys*

Where gratefulness gathers,
blessings flow.

*Treasure & Keys*

From her pitcher she poured compassion, but there was also an unexpected strength which came from enchanted swords and dragon fire.

*Treasure & Keys*

As we talk through our own stories
and reflect on what we've learned,
we often answer our own questions.

*Treasure & Keys*

When you awaken to life, life awakens to you.
When you awaken to love, love awakens to you.

*Treasure & Keys*

In everyone's (unknown) tests and battles are keys of light, lit by love, always ready to guide them.

In silence and surrender they are discovered. Releasing what is false creates space for healing.

*Treasure & Keys*

# Suffering & Shadow

I found out the hard way that I couldn't trust people I thought I could.

But I also know there are trustworthy people in the world.

*Suffering & Shadow*

Do you ever notice that many 'Christian' people seem to be very judgmental? Which means they are not loving their neighbor, one of the biggest parts of Christ's message(s)?

Do you suppose that if they are kept in guilt and fear and shame, that perhaps they don't love themselves, and could that be why they don't love their neighbor(s), even though they are extensions of God?

If they are holding things against themselves, maybe that is why they hold things against others. If they do not love themselves, due to the false or incomplete teachings of organized religion, then perhaps that is why they often treat their brothers and sisters in such abominable, judgmental ways.

This is only food for thought, intended to bring awareness by presenting a different perspective. If anyone has been treated poorly by a so-called Christians or has witnessed it, they will know EXACTLY what I am speaking of here. This is simply a message. Peace and blessings to all on your journeys. There comes a time to recognize we are love.

*Suffering & Shadow*

His feelings were deep like the ocean but he feared their depths, so he hid from them in a bottle.

*Suffering & Shadow*

How deep his suffering went,
she did not know. It was time
to pull some weeds.

*Suffering & Shadow*

It is said that the best gift you can give another person is simply to include them. And similarly, that is exactly how some people hurt others, to not include them, to shun them.

It is that treatment from someone I cared about very deeply, which sent me on the path I am on today of healing the collective.

What we perceive, real or imagined, directs and redirects us. What we gain or create from it is up to us.

*Suffering & Shadow*

He wanted to be a savior of
certain people, but he didn't
realize they had to do their
own work. No co-dependency.

*Suffering & Shadow*

Sometimes when you 'vote' to get rid of one piece of shit thing, you end up with another. Welcome to our world.

Nothing is perfect here. Let's not pretend that it ever will be. However, it gets closer to perfect when people stop being haters and victims.

We can be proactive in positive ways and make a positive difference, but we can't do it from negative energy and negative thought forms and loops which are connected to invisible shackles

*Suffering & Shadow*

# Whispers from the Heart

If we feel we can trust no one, it might be because we've had to close ourselves off due to being hurt, in an effort to protect ourselves from further hurt, or so we think.

It is wise to be wary, but we cannot heal with a closed heart.

*Whispers from the Heart*

Love, and how we perceive it or misperceive it, is an interesting thing.

The way people feel something they can't describe.

A glimpse of something more, they're always drawn back to.

*Whispers from the Heart*

Poetry is code talk of and
for the heart and soul.

*Whispers from the Heart*

It's a stanza,
not a novel,
but it's powerful.

*Whispers from the Heart*

The fire in my heart glowed
fiercely when it was kindled
by him.

*Whispers from the Heart*

We are not supposed to hide our light under a bushel. A bushel of false guilt, shame, fear and lies. Lies could also mean misinterpretations and things purposefully tweaked which are now 'believed' to be truth.

This work is for true seekers, those who are ready to step out of their boxes and programming, or for those who already have, who understand things on deeper or higher levels. For the awakening. For awareness.

*Whispers from the Heart*

Something about his energy, his essence, whispered to part of me that remembered him and my heart opened and embraced him.

*Whispers of the Heart*

# Light through the Cracks

If they won't listen, you have to leave them where they are. Speak or write your peace, then take care of you.

*Light through the Cracks*

When we notice that we no longer make openly snide or derogatory remarks or comments about another, because there are no similar thoughts which precede it, then we might be able to notice where we have healed or risen above something lower.

When we resent another, it is reflecting something unresolved or unhealed within us.

*Light through the Cracks*

That moment when a pinpoint of light becomes a beacon of brilliance.

*Light through the Cracks*

My armor became too heavy
so I had to leave it behind.

Armor of light replaced it.

*Light through the Cracks*

A friend posed a question. He asked, 'Do extreme circumstances create an empath, or is it their misfortune to be born into horribly abusive situations? Is that the fire, anvil, and hammer that forms us?'

I replied, 'A very good question and situations likely differ. Most empaths are probably born with empathic ability but it's honed through the gauntlet of initiations and suffering.

If we are born into horribly abusive situations, it's because we agreed to it on a spiritual level. It might sound crazy, but it's either to balance karma, to learn, to evolve and/or to ascend.

We also have ongoing ancestral issues. Patterns which need to be broken and wounds which need to behealed.'

*Light through the Cracks*

We can't always control our reactions
when unhealed things come raging out.

*Light through the Cracks*

A friend commented that it's amazing how sacred knowledge can be distorted. Another friend said it has to do with how our upbringing has shaped us and of the importance of accepting others for who they are.

I replied that sacred knowledge is different to and for everyone, due to what we have learned or opened to from different experiences and different perceptions.

Two people walking down the same path are not having the same experience. To share perspectives and learn is divine. To try to put others down in resentment and resistance is often from woundedness, stuckness and/or ego running the show.

Distorted sacred knowledge is what religions have evolved into today, and yes, programming and conditioning are or can be, shackles. When we move beyond it, is because we are or were open enough to do so. It is because we recognize and embrace our sacred divinity.

*Light through the Cracks*

At first the light might be blinding and uncomfortable. We have to adjust to its brilliance. We must remember from whence we came.

*Light through the Cracks*

# Spoken from the Soul

He loved deeply and quietly. He didn't communicate it openly very much or very often. There were parts of him which were frozen.

*Spoken from the Soul*

He said to me, "Explain to me what your soul desires."

I answered, "I will attempt to describe it to the best of my ability through my limited awareness. It is connections like I am about to describe that have brought much more awareness to my life and that awareness is always growing, but never complete.

I don't even like to use the word 'desire', but perhaps my soul craves reconnection of the deepest, closest kind.

It's something hard to explain and extremely rare and difficult to find and maintain, due to wounds and fears. People block it, even though they don't mean to.

Some deep part of my soul enjoys and is kindled by in-depth conversations about life and what is beyond this life. Discussions on remembering our divinity.

To be able to be fully myself, no matter how powerful or weak. To be open. To flow. To be heard. To make a positive difference. To learn. To remember.

151

I love what can be created with words through intention and higher vibration. Also, I like comfortable silence. Things known without being spoken. Patience. Familiarity. Celebration of small things. Awakening. Observing and acknowledging the beauty of nature. Wisdom recognized in certain books, recognized by the soul.

The touch between two people in recognition and honor of a deep spiritual connection, is electric. When they are fully engaged with one another and can honor that to the highest degree, to the degree that each is nurtured and fed and lifted and healed and loved. Where nothing can interfere. But fears must be put aside.

To express that depth of love and connection through touch, with the right person, where soul recognizes soul, and soul honors soul, is beyond words or anything words might attempt to describe or imply.

When one person drawn to another like a moth to a flame and engages the other in a way no other does or can, its true magnetism. It crackles.

But if the spiritual connection isn't there, for me, it cannot and does not have that depth of meaning and it's not something my soul is drawn toward.

That being must engage me in a way my which my heart and soul recognizes, because that person recognizes me on a level deeper than I recognize myself.

I love it when someone sees me deeply and shows me myself in a new light, because part of me is in them, and part of them is in me. That is what speaks to my heart and soul."

He said, "I love your spirit, I love what I can see in you."

*Spoken from the Soul*

Through the mists, home awaits and is rediscovered through courage, patience and grace.

*Spoken from the Soul*

He told her he saw her brilliance, that he saw the light of her being. He said it was like Old Testament descriptions of seeing God or angels. He was shown what he had sensed and known all about her along.

He experienced a unified connection with her, not experienced in this earthly realm. He said he couldn't explain why his soul suddenly opened and breathed her essence in.

*Spoken from the Soul*

He said, "I have immense respect for you and your deep passion for the esoteric and the mystical. I feel your intense energy and your sincerity and authenticity. You are direct and unvarnished and that makes you very attractive to me."

She replied, "You recognize my soul."

*Spoken from the Soul*

I said to him, 'I'm sorry you are suffering so much.
I hope you can find some relief that isn't tied to
any side or ideology.

It must be horrible to hate someone or something
so much. I hope you find peace and truth within
yourself which is where it always resides.

Truth and happiness are not dependent on things
outside of ourselves and until we discover that
and awaken to it, we suffer greatly and often
cause others to as well.

When we stop reacting to incompleteness we
might begin to discover truth.

*Spoken from the Soul*

# Beyond Belief

The dragon in me smiled
when I began to remember
who I Am.

*Beyond Belief*

He wouldn't let her have the version of him which was free of the effects of alcohol, so her experience with him wasn't with the man, it was with the mask.

It was tainted. It was a triangle with what the alcohol let in. The booze and whatever that demon was, won, and he and she lost.

Beyond Belief

He didn't tell her he thought she was beautiful or what she really meant to him. But someone else did.

*Beyond Belief*

Time is used for the purposes we wrote into the matrix realm of illusion. Much of what we 'believe' is not accurate or complete.

That is for each person to discover individually, if it's meant to be for them on this journey, whether they become true seekers, or not.

There are many distractions and the biggest one is usually fear and fear is usually a liar.

*Beyond Belief*

Certain events break us away from patterns in life which don't serve us, to direct us toward our highest and best good... if we are open enough to recognize blessings in disguise, before or after the fact.

*Beyond Belief*

Wild fires burned my house to the ground and that is part of what redirected me to do what I'm doing now, to my calling as a messenger to help heal the collective.

Not everything that appears to be devastation really is. It's not what it appears, at least not at first. It might be redirection, to blessings, to callings, to being of better service to humanity. It depends on where our souls are called or what they are called to.

The good that comes from the bad. But it depends on our perspective and whether or not we break out of boxes and break patterns which don't serve us.

*Beyond Belief*

We volunteer for missions here to fix what is messed up, through love, knowledge, wisdom, and remembering.

Functioning in this lower dimension is or can be very difficult. There separation and/or the illusion of it.

*Beyond Belief*

# Metaphoric Light

When the light entered,
new worlds were revealed.

*Metaphoric Light*

Jesus tells us we don't need an intermediary. We don't need priests, we don't need the church to be complete, 'saved', or connected to God. Much of what is understood and taught through churches is incomplete. He tells us the kingdom is within. He tells us, "Seek and ye shall find."

If a person hasn't studied in depth, from various sources, including and especially within, then they might not find deeper answers and truths which resonate with their soul. Truths which are far different from anything 'organized religions' are selling.

*Metaphoric Light*

Religions like to allow us to believe we are 'sinners', that we are somehow bad or wrong. But we are of God, so how can that be? Maybe that depends on which god people are identifying with.

We can be off track or off course which is what 'to sin' actually means. The correct translation of 'to sin' means to miss the point or to miss the mark.

Wouldn't it make more sense to help people be in a positive vibration of love, healing, and acceptance of self, and to be healthily available to serve humanity, rather than to attempt to shackle them to darkness through falsehood?

We must be aware of what darkness and ignorance feed on.

*Metaphoric Light*

She began to notice that so many people were too wounded to contribute to a nurturing relationship. Maybe she was too.

*Metaphoric Light*

Words are powerful. We are the Word. How wonderful when we realize we really are not separate.

*Metaphoric Light*

I recognize that in the mystery of your sacred code, that there is a message for me. There is recognition of me. There is compassion for me. There is love for me. Thank you.

*Metaphoric Light*

Surrounded by native beauty with the energy of the animals surrounding her, she shined a protective, special light all around her which radiated out beyond the physical realm.

The light was the magic of love. It incinerated and transmuted darker, lower energies of pain, suffering and ignorance.

*Metaphoric Light*

# Perspectives

Falling in love might be an aspect of recognizing part of yourself in another. Something you're drawn to that you can't explain and don't quite understand or yet remember.

Soul connections. Allowing yourself to love and be loved. A reflection of the love you are. The love you see in another is in you.

*Perspectives*

She stood with the lion, or so it appeared. The lion was part of her, usually hidden. Only the very intuitive and in tune could sense or see it.

*Perspectives*

When I became a true seeker and began to study religions, the more I learned about man-made religions and all of the faults and incompleteness they contain, they less I liked them. Or, the less they resonated with me if I wanted a more pure connection with Source.

I discovered I don't need them because they keep so many people stuck in guilt and shame and fear which is darkness working through them. Christ is a very high vibrational energy which has worked through certain beings through history. What was taught millennia ago has been misunderstood greatly by mankind.

It's okay to have a connection and relationship with Jesus without being shackled to the falsehoods of religion(s). Christ, the energy of Christ, is love. It is in all of us and we don't have to join a religion and jump through hoops to access it.

*Perspectives*

As we soldier on through the rain storms of life, things are always growing, getting ready to blossom.

*Perspectives*

.

Power in the name of Jesus. Yes, there is that, and some very intuitive people can feel the amazing vibration of it and what it connects to. I have intuitive friends who are not religious at all and they have great love and respect and honor for Jesus, who is also one of many Ascended Masters.

Some have been greatly harmed by the effects or ill-effects of man-made religions. They have discovered and/or determined that something is missing or that something is inaccurate or incomplete.

From my limited perspective, anyone who consciously moves away from religion because they recognize its falsehood or incompleteness, or that it is holding them back, is awake or awakening.

However, if we hold onto hatred and resistance, and put people down who aren't where we are, then we aren't quite there yet. We can be aware of what religions are or are not, without having to put them or people down. We can also speak of what has deep meaning to us for awareness. Sometimes we are guided to do so.

Some speak of a false god. To speak of the false god is very interesting and very deep and is a thing, but it has nothing to do with Jesus and/or the Christ who came to try to awaken people to it. It is way beyond that.

When someone takes the time and responsibility to become a true seeker and study with an open mind and heart, not connected to and/or clinging to ideologies which often make up part of our identity, they might learn the following:

It is understood from many ancient scriptures, that the false god is jealous, wrathful and vengeful because it is incomplete and did not know it wasn't the high god. It manipulates mankind, and it uses religions to do it. Misinterpretations of religious scriptures.

Some feel, as they did at the time of Jesus, that darkness plays that and feeds off of it. When we recognize that we are not separate and rise above the ideologies of separation, religion, politics, hatred, jealousy and wrath, then we rise back toward truth. Rising into the Sacred Heart or dropping into it. Centeredness.

Religions might, or typically do, contain parts of truth, but they are all tweaked and twisted by mankind, due to misinterpretation and mistranslation.

It is said if you truly want to understand scriptures as accurately as possible, you need to learn the language they were written in, as much has been lost in translation. There are words in the original, ancient languages, which there are no English words for.

Image how it could end up being tweaked due to being misunderstood, and it has. One example is that in the ancient languages, there were masculine and feminine words, and in the ancient languages, the Holy Spirit was always referred to in the Feminine. So why is it then, that the Orthodox Church later changed it to be masculine?

Like everything, it's really both, but which part is speaking? The imbalanced incompleteness of patriarchal religions is coming into the light.
Fear is a liar. Sin means to miss the point or to miss the mark. Churches are money making businesses. They control through fear and ignorance. This is known to many and unknown to many others.

We are all tested here to find our truth within, the kingdom within, which Jesus, and/or the Christ working through him, spoke of.

Jesus was teaching sacred Mystery School teachings in code, parables, for those with ears to hear. This is what is meant by don't throw pearls to the swine. You don't share sacred spiritual wisdom with the sleeping, they won't understand it, and it is sacred wisdom to be honored and protected, not perverted.

Only when they are awakening are they ready to receive or open to the knowledge and truth that is already in them.

Religions are meant to point toward God which is in in each being. Many don't even realize how God is in each being. People are programmed to think or believe they are separate from God or that God is separate from them. They are programmed to feel unworthy which is an atrocity against God. We are of God and no part of God is unworthy. Again, that might depend on what god a person worships.

As Buddha said, 'The finger pointing at the moon is not the moon." Religions are not God nor do they fully understand what God is. None of us really can understand or remember what God is in this lower vibrational realm of amnesia and ignorance.

We are here to ascend and we have to move beyond belief to do it. We must do the work ourselves. We must have our own awakenings and that typically happens through the hardships which crack us open to allow the light to get in, and out.

Jesus never wanted or intended to be a religion or to be perceived as a god. That was man who misinterpreted and mistranslated scripture. The notion of the rapture is an interpretation that is only about 200 years old and NOT what the original followers of Jesus' teachings believed.

But most Christians don't know that because they haven't taken responsibility for what they claim to believe. They have not studied nearly enough. They rely on someone else to do their work for them which is not why we came here.

Forces of darkness would like nothing better than for people not to do the work necessary to ascend, so it can continue to feed off the suffering of humanity, especially through religions and politics.

Many study the Bible, and only the Bible, with their collective, cliquey, self-righteous groups, endeavoring to judge others and put them down to make themselves feel superior. It is false.

Memorizing scripture and then throwing it at people in self-righteous judgment is nothing but ego. Overactive, overinflated ego on a lower or lost path. Jesus did not claim to be a god nor is he claiming to be a god. That was/is mankind.

Just because he was sent by God, by an energy which most of mankind cannot and does not understand, doesn't mean he wanted or intended to be worshipped. Many people worship in honor of his great love and their love for him.

God, the High God, is not a bearded man in the sky who is jealous, vengeful and wrathful, who doesn't acknowledge his feminine counterpart. Per many ancient scriptures, the High God is not the god of the Old Testament.

185

The High God doesn't have any need or reason to put people in fear or keep them in fear to control them. It, He/She, is not so weak or manipulative to require suffering. If we suffer, it suffers as it is in all of us.

The early followers of Jesus believed the God who sent Christ was not the god of the Old Testament. They felt the High God sent Christ to help humanity get unstuck which included not being so wrapped up in their religion and falsities they were not recognizing. That's what he was doing.

The energy of the High God is not only masculine. It is androgynous, both masculine and feminine, it has to be. All higher divine beings are androgynous, they have male and female counterparts. Balanced. What god would be so afraid of the feminine that it would squash her? It makes no sense.

God is a vast energy which cannot be labeled, named, described or understand by the human conscious mind. Want to glimpse God? Go into your heart space for a start.

Disconnect from ideologies and the false notion of separation.

The above is a limited perspective from limited interpretations and much study to date of something very deep and very vast which most beings here have forgotten their connection to.

It is shared here for the purpose to get people to think and to move beyond thinking and into remembering what they already know.

Peace and blessings and may you continue to be in awe of the wonders all around and be open enough to recognize blessings when they present, even in disguise.

*Perspectives*

We hold the pain of our past days,
Hoping it will fade away,
The pain it comes, the pain it goes,
As long as we're traveling down this road,

None of us will ever be the same,
They tell me to leave, but I'm going to stay,
I'm gonna stand tall, so they can't bring me down,
I'm lost in my mind, but I'll be found.

I'm covering all the scars,
From my thoughts of my past that were in the
dark,
But now that I've found the light inside of me,
I'm gonna choose to be happy.

K.P. Age 11

# ABOUT THE AUTHOR

Janine Palmer (Spirit Silver Moon) grew up in Northern California and resides in Southern California today. After devastating county-wide wild fires in Southern California and global economic collapse, Janine and her family endured physical, economical and emotional losses, along with the loss of friendships.

Judgmental treatment by so-called religious people (family/friends) caused her to question religions due to poor treatment by others in religious ideology. These initiations tested her inner strength and caused her to investigate more deeply for truth, what brings true happiness, forward movement, the evolvement of the soul and ultimately she discovered her calling.

She was a phoenix who rose from her own ashes with a powerful story to share of truth, strength, wisdom, compassion, love and taking one's power back. We must remember our magnificence to in order to rise above so much illusion. Looking for answers, Janine Palmer (Silver Moon) extensively studied and continues to study multiple healing modalities for emotional and spiritual healing.

Janine has studied World Religions, Spirituality, Early Christianity, Gnosticism, Philosophy, Critical Thinking, Biblical Scholars, and Spiritual teachers. Janine is a Clinical Hypnotherapist and Shamanic Practitioner.

In the spiritual and emotional arenas, Janine has studied and become certified in the following areas: Cognitive Behavioral Hypnotherapy, Ericksonian Hypnosis, Energy Psychology, Emotional Freedom Technique (EFT or Tapping), Kinesiology, Muscle Testing, Neuro-linguistic Programming (NLP) the language of the mind, Reiki Master and Gamma Healing for overcoming energy vampires, healing emotional traumas, anxiety, depression and PTSD, and Shamanic Journey Work.

These modalities are helpful for releasing stress, old pain, resentment, anger, doubt, grief, unforgiveness or anything which blocks forward movement. Through her healing sessions, whether held in person, via phone or skype, she has helped others heal, grow, overcome obstacles and move forward lighter after releasing what no longer serves. This knowledge and wisdom is contained within her writings of uplifting messages for healing. She shares tools we can use to assist ourselves and others on their path. Janine is the author of multiple books containing many genres and messages from various teachings and modalities. The four main genres are story poems, romance, rising above dogma and emotional and spiritual healing. These are presented as poetic tales which have received very positive support and feedback around the world.

Janine's compassion and calling to help others break free of limiting and painful situations can be felt through the writings contained her he book series Divine Heretic. She does God's work for humanity, for the collective and greater good. It is a gift and a blessing she is very grateful for.

59421497R00115

Made in the USA
Middletown, DE
11 August 2019